MANITOBA

SPRING

The prairie crocus appears like a welcoming spring breeze after a solemn snowy sleep. Quick to herald the changing season, it signals the reawakening of life. Its radiant blooms make a mockery of winter's vain threats and bear witness to the strength of gentle flowers. Soft feathered buds flock together, each waiting their turn to mirror the sun with their yellow faces. Not far behind the crocus, canoeing enthusiasts move onto lakes, rivers, streams and rivulets just melted in search of the new life spring brings.

MANITOBA

Edited and compiled by Irvin Kroeker

Published by

WHITECAP BOOKS LTD.,
Suite 1, 431 Mountain Hwy.
North Vancouver, B.C.
V7J 2L1

First Edition 1979
Second (Revised) Edition 1982

Copyright © 1979 Whitecap Books

ISBN 0-920620-07-8 (paperback)
ISBN 0-920620-08-6 (hardcover)

Printed in Canada

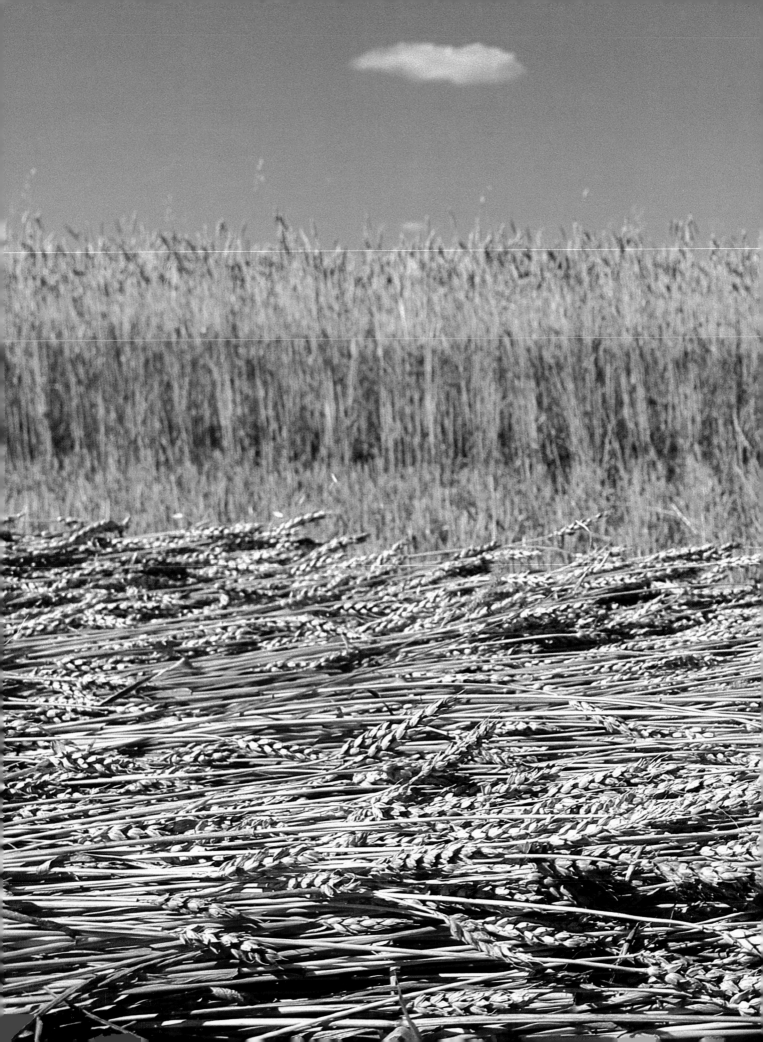

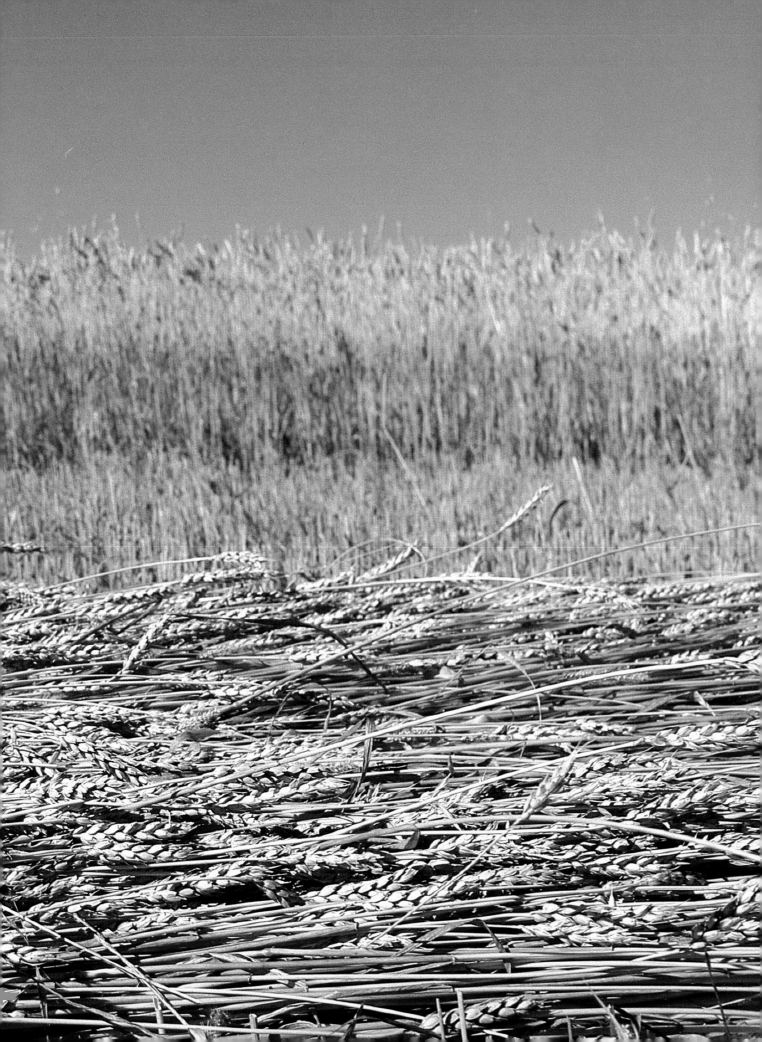

SUMMER

The beaches are filled with laughing children, as sunlight warms the countryside. Out in the woods, young wildlife learns the way of survival. Summer is that time when the symphony of the seasons explodes. In cities and towns around the province people celebrate the fat of the land and the ways of their forebears with fun-filled festivals that bring city folk and country folk together. The sway of grainstalks in gentle evening breezes can often be heard in ripening golden fields as sunlight, and occasional rains, prepare them for harvest.

Foreword

"Manitoba" is a book of affection for a province in its many dimensions. It is not a book of history nor a sociological study though the text and photographs show the best of Manitoba. It is purely and simply a bouquet, a picture-fragrance-recapturing of a special place . . . Manitoba and special people . . . Manitobans.

Pearl Mc Gonigal

Lieutenant Governor of the Province of Manitoba.

AUTUMN

The crops have been harvested and stored, fall plowing ends and the trees turn to crimson as leaves freeze and gently drift. Some days are already chilly, others are still warm, and then an Indian summer lingers on to delay a week or two the arrival of snow. Burning stubble beside rural roads sends pleasant aromas wafting across the countryside. Fishermen know that now is a good angling time. Hunters prepare for their annual treks through the hills. Fowl suppers and Thanksgiving feasts bring out the best of Mom's cooking. And then the leaves all fall, leaving the trees bare for winter.

Credits

The Writers

Hames, Jill: "Manitoba Legacy" on page 26; "Regions of Manitoba" on page 34; and "The Arts" on page 68. Pasta, Victor: "Sports and Recreation" on page 58. Kroeker, Diane: "Wildlife" on page 50. Kroeker, Irvin: "The People" on page 18; and "The Parks" on page 42.

The Photographers

John Addison, Hugh Allan, Jerry Anderson, Bob Armstrong, Paul Chipman, David Fox/University of Winnipeg, Ken Frazer, Edward W. Gifford, Kathryn Gillis, Kenn Green, Colin Hay, Henry Kalen, Cory Kilbert, Paul Kostas, J. A. Kraulis, Dave Landy, Ernest Mayer, Alan McTavish, Ted Muir, Wes Pascoe, Victor Pasta, Simon Popov, Prairie Hotelman/Hugh Allan, Rawsthorne and Charter, Jan Simonson, John Lewis, John Sundra, James Whan, Richard T. Wright.

Printed and Bound
by

DWFriesen & Sons Ltd.

Altona, Manitoba, Canada

WINTER

Manitoba's winter descends gently, a smooth tran-
sition from the blazing colours of autumn to the
subtle hues of winter. When the snow first flies it
transforms the countryside into a world of fantasy
and mysterious new shapes. There is nothing like
fresh snow piled high on dark-green spruce trees
to entice you outdoors in search of picturesque
beauty. Ice at the riverbanks and lakeshores creeps
out across the water. Nature creates fascinating
sculptures. When the cold season has settled in
well, snowmobiles bring laughing families
out to enjoy this winter wonderland.

Contents

◁ *Tom Barrow of Swan River reads the family's treasured old Bible, printed in 1620, a valued heirloom.*

△ *Voyageur for several years, Gérard Prenovault of St. Boniface wears the garb of his historical counterparts.*

The People

Manitoba's population is a fascinating collection of individual people. More in Manitoba than probably anywhere else in the world, they hold onto their heritages, proud of their distinctive old-world backgrounds. In 20th-century Canada, Manitobans live in the middle.

Manitobans are a lovable lot. They are fiercely proud of the traditions their forefathers handed down to them; vivacious; sometimes cantankerous; politically opinionated; and friendly.

They have carved for themselves a lifestyle that is both old and new. Picture a bearded Hutterite with a name that dates back to the 16th-century Reformation, who on Sun-

day sings hymns as old as his name, but who Monday morning, climbs into his perch atop the most modern combine to harvest a field of golden grain that is planted, nurtured and cut according to all the latest research he has studied. This man is just as much a Manitoban, just as friendly and hospitable if you take the time to go out and meet him, as the bank manager living next door.

The people of Manitoba have all the occupations of every other province or state in the world, and many of them are lucky enough to be working at jobs they really like. Sure, they complain. They constantly gripe about the weather and they always wish, six months after an election,

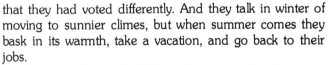

that they had voted differently. And they talk in winter of moving to sunnier climes, but when summer comes they bask in its warmth, take a vacation, and go back to their jobs.

Getting to know Manitobans is never real until you get to know individual people. When I think of the individuals it has been my privilege to know, the characterization statistics fall flat, and the personalities of real people come to life.

There's a fine salt-of-the-earth old gentleman in Grand-view. The day I met him, he was on the cold cement floor, legs stiff with arthritis, painting a showcase in the town's

△ *Clockwise from top left. Train conductor taking a break at Wabowden; Banjo player at Souris; a young girl smiles in winter; a girl on the merry-go-round at the Russell Fair.*

◁ *Woodcarver Alex Bloodworth cuts intricately designed figures into panels of wood that people bring him.*

△ *Clockwise from top left. A secretary, Kris Buschau spends weekends skydiving; two farmers reminiscing at the Austin Threshermen's Reunion; Terry Smythe of Winnipeg, checking one of the numerous old music machines he has restored; a miner fighting to be king at Thompson's Nickel Days.*

new museum to hold for his community's children and grandchildren the homesteading treasures he had collected during his 80-odd years. His name is Watson Crossley.

In Winnipeg lives a kind, slightly eccentric nurse who has written an award-winning novel about her family, which includes a well-known botanist and an artist. They lived north of the Assiniboine River near Treesbank. Her name is Alma Criddle, and what a delight it is to share with her an occasional cup of tea. She, too, is a Manitoban who sends all stereotyping attempts flying properly out the window.

Winnipeg is filled with wonderful people, a mixture of descendants from businessmen, politicians, labourers, ar-

△ *Town businessmen take an active part in dishing out corn-on-the-cob during Morden's Corn and Apple Days, which usually end Manitoba's summer festival season.*

tisans and farmers. The women are chic, the men handsomely dressed.

To get a taste of country living, get yourself invited to a farm one day. Once there, it doesn't take long until you're helping with the chores while discussing anything from solar eclipses to provincial politics. And that's where you get a taste of the world's undisputed best in country cooking and downright fine hospitality.

Religious holidays are times when old-world traditions provincial people still hold dear surface the most. Ukrainians chant age-old masses. Even if you're not one of them, you get a lump in your throat when you see an urban

◁ *A young Mennonite girl from Altona is already an old hand at eating the sunflower seeds grown extensively in the area where she lives during the annual Sunflower Festival.*

△ *The cattle auction at Dauphin where buyers bid for some of Manitoba's finest stock.*

family walking into church, preparing to worship together in a language even the youngsters speak.

And then there are the French-Canadians. Who can resist trying to lay claim to at least a bit of French blood when the bells of St. Boniface Cathedral salute the Voyageur in February? I tend to look at French Canadian girls in Manitoba through very romantic eyes. Daughters of hardy, fun-loving folk, I call them.

Once I met a poet. Actually, the first time I saw him, he was reciting at Gimli's Icelandic Festival, and I didn't even talk to him then. But two years later, by chance, I drove onto his farm south of Morden without realizing it was his

place. I recognized him after he came out. Following introductions, he invited me and my family into his big kitchen for some coffee and punch, and then unravelled for us his tender love for the poetic sagas of Icelandic people. His name is Paul Sigurdson. He, too, has his own unique characteristics.

For every person symbolically mentioned here, there are hundreds more, and hundreds more again — a million in all. Each one has an individual tale to tell; each one has a hobby, a heartache, a history and a future. I love them all, and the reason why is because they are the provincial people amongst whom I belong. ☐

26

◁ *Turn-of-the 20th-century poster lured immigrants to Manitoba to come and tame the prairies.*

△ *Rebuilt five times, the St. Boniface Basilica is an historic structure where the Red and Assiniboine meet.*

Manitoba Legacy

Everyone has roots. The people of Manitoba have roots that stretch back to the British Isles, Continental Europe, Iceland, Russia and Asia. When our parents and grandparents made the momentous decision to leave their homelands and sail for Canada with its promise of endless prairie, they packed not only their belongings, but their heritages as well.

The fledgling province of Manitoba was soon populated with hard-working families, and became rich in a variety of old-world cultures. Of course, in the early days it was important to be Canadian, whatever that may have been. It was important not to be different in this country, which had saved so many from poverty and persecution. The special celebrations and revered religious holidays were certainly observed, although unobtrusively, and favourite delicacies were prepared only at home.

Assimilation did its slow and steady work over the years, but fortunately this didn't mean losing a heritage as much as finding an identity. The preoccupation with being and feeling Canadian diminished in a young country where every man could find security if he worked hard enough. Manitobans eventually came full circle, and it was time to look back and rediscover their beginnings. After some retrospection, people made some very careful observations.

△ Ledgers of the famed and historical Hudson's Bay Company are now in the Manitoba Archives.

△ Blacksmith at Lower Fort Garry, a national historic site, talks with visitors as if living 100 years ago.

△ Two youngsters sample the food of their forefathers at Gimli's Islendingadagurinn, the Icelandic Festival.

△ *Fort la Reine Museum near Portage la Prairie is on the trail that led from Winnipeg northwest across the prairies to the Rockies. It is a village museum, bringing yesteryear to life.*

△ *Historic Lower Fort Garry, the original home of the western Canadian fur trade.*

△ Grotto beside Church of the Immaculate Conception at Cook's Creek is the destination point for an annual pilgrimage of Manitoba Christians each August.

▷ Ukrainian Church near St. John's Park, Winnipeg.

and found some new perspectives. They did some digging and liked what they saw.

What better way to share their pride than with a festival? The town of Dauphin now throws open its doors for Canada's National Ukrainian Festival, a wild week of folk dancing and cossacks. The Manitoba Highland Gathering at Selkirk brings together the finest of pipes, drums and dancers and Steinbach's Pioneer Days relive the straight-laced ways of early Mennonite settlers.

Fête Franco-Manitobaine at La Broquerie honours the French-Canadian patron Saint Jean Baptiste with fine fiddling and hearty food. The people of Gimli, focal point of

◁ *An aerial view of the Assiniboine River in western Manitoba.*

△ *A field of canola west of Winnipeg.*

the largest Icelandic community outside the mother country itself, pay tribute to their hardy Viking ancestry with Islendingadagurinn. The Indian people of Manitoba, whose roots are the deepest and have been tested the most, reaffirm their age-old histories and strengths at The Pas during Opasquia Indian Days.

There are festivals that relive the adventure and hardship of settling a new country. York Boat Days at Norway House remind us of the cumbersome hand-hewn craft that sailed Lake Winnipeg carrying everything from fur-trading supplies to Selkirk settlers. The Threshermen's Reunion at Austin brings back the days of sodbusters.

The roots which those first pioneers put down into the soil have grown strong. Morden has corn and apples; Russell beef and barley; and Altona sunflowers. Their respective festivals celebrate the fat of the land. The Flin Flon Trout Festival and Thompson's Nickel Days grew out of surrounding natural resources.

Our festivals share age-old customs and mouth-watering cuisine of more than 50 cultures. They give people a chance to sing and dance and celebrate the good life of our province. They say who we are, where we have come from and what we have done. Most of all, they tell us that the roots have taken. ☐

◁ *Autumn's blazing colour brings the Red's riverbanks to the close of another growing season.*

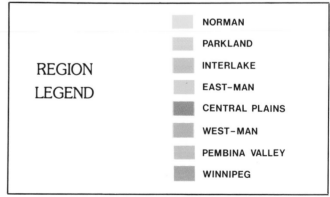

REGION LEGEND

NORMAN

PARKLAND

INTERLAKE

EAST–MAN

CENTRAL PLAINS

WEST–MAN

PEMBINA VALLEY

WINNIPEG

△ *Residence of the Lieutenant-Governor of Manitoba at No. 10 Kennedy Street with Legislative Building in background.*

Regions of Manitoba

Manitoba's eight regions best represent the geographic and economic areas of the province. A tidy, official statement of fact, perhaps, but one that can't possibly convey the rich histories and cultural heritages that do, in fact, set Norman, Parkland, West-Man, Central Plains, Pembina Valley, Interlake, East-Man and Winnipeg, apart from each other.

Norman has been the backbone of the province for centuries. Its colourful history is a jumble of Indian tribal rivalries, Hudson's Bay Company explorers, bush pilots and priests. Even today, northerners tell stories of medicine men, hermit trappers and sled-dog racers. More likely,

they'll want to talk about the lumbercamps, upstart mining towns and powerful hydro-electric plants that have given Norman a strong new voice in the future of Manitoba.

The northern half of East-Man shares some of the history of Norman and much of its geography. Its cold, little-known lakes are edged by miles of trackless forest. Ancient, scarred cliffs rear high above silent rivers. Perfect solitude, precambrian country's finest natural resource.

But solitude is not a word heard often in the southwestern portion of East-Man. Like all the other southern regions, people are just too busy planting crops and tending their small, thriving businesses. Ask folks from

Steinbach to Brandon to tell you a story about their region and they'll recall the days of sodbusters as they proudly display their museums crammed with memorabilia of homesteading. The nationalities may differ — Ukrainian, Mennonite, French-Canadian, English, Scottish, German or Icelandic — but the tales of adventure, heartbreak and prosperity are the same. Their legacy to their children, a good life on the plains and the valleys of southern Manitoba, is a testimony to their faith in the Lord and an honest day's work.

The tough prairie grasslands of the Central Plains, which once fed the buffalo and now fatten cattle and yield

△ *Old and new architecture along Broadway Avenue, Winnipeg.*

◁ *The Canadian Mint in St. Boniface.*

their promise of rich harvests are a far cry from the wild marshes and lumpy, stone-strewn fields of the Interlake. And then, the abandoned fishing villages of the Interlake are, in turn, worlds apart from the Pembina Valley with its rolling hills, corn and sunflower fields, and apple orchards.

West-Man is seamed by the meandering Assiniboine River, silent witness to the caravans of covered wagons that once camped along its banks. On its eastern border, this region boasts a sand desert, and scattered throughout the area like dimes are tiny lakes that once watered thirsty livestock, and now welcome vacationing farmers in camper trailers. To the north, the Parkland region, Manitoba's last

△ The prairie crocus, Manitoba's official flower, is first to bloom each spring as snow is still melting away.

◁ The coastal region of Hudson Bay is entirely different from any other in the province. Here the Anglican Church of Churchill sits on a foundation of rock overlooking the bay.

△ *Rich with a variety of crops, the Red River Valley has been immortalized in song. Here a yellow field of sunflowers near Altona brings vibrant colour to a background of lush trees in which a farm nestles.*

agricultural frontier, has also become a verdant playground, its wooded hills and pothole lakes perfect for year-round recreation.

Manitoba's eighth region is its smallest, and its best-known, although there are a few oldtimers who can remember when Winnipeg was just another dusty frontier town. Its history is peopled with revolutionaries, archbishops, millionaires and thousands of immigrants who sought the familiarity of neighborhoods like the "Foreign Quarter" before venturing into spheres of business and politics to make their dreams come true. As a result, Winnipeg has become a unique cosmopolitan place.

EMBLEMS

Top. Coat of Arms
Above. Manitoba Seal
Below. The Tartan

Her structures are leaving a legacy of history. The St. Boniface Museum has been, at different times, a hospital, a school and an orphange, while the Winnipeg Mint is a flashy new edifice designed to symbolize a storehouse for grain. The old and the new stand side by side. Old bank buildings in the financial district are flanked by the City Hall complex and the Centennial Centre, a mecca for the arts.

In the end it is the citizens of Winnipeg, along with the good people of Manitoba's other seven regions, who have made their corners of the province just a little different from the town down the road, and just as nice a place in which to live. □

△ *Upper. Shoreline of Lake Winnipeg can be a tranquil scene one day, tumultous the next because of storms that build and blow.*

△ *Lower. Crimson barns and white farmhouses make going home to the country a pleasure each time.*

◁ *Pine trees and maples grow side by side to bring Manitobans a kaleidoscope of colour each fall in the parks, be they in the city or out in the country.*

▽ *In the middle of the prairie is a desert, located near Carberry, the heart of Spruce Woods Provincial Park.*

▷ *Footbridge in Spruce Woods Park leads across the Assiniboine River in an area where swimming and camping are popular all summer long.*

The Parks

Parks are for people. They are places where the inviting beauty of Manitoba's sometimes lush, sometimes stark and strong country is preserved for people who like being outdoors.

When you look at a highway map, you see them as patches of green, but when you follow a road through an entrance gate, you begin experiencing firsthand the unique geography of each park you visit. It brings out the adventure in you. Discovering historical sites or naturally beautiful places along the way gives you a hint of what explorers must have felt when they first came upon some of the spectacular sites the parks embrace.

Take Spruce Woods Park. Nestled there in the trees is a small, ecologically fragile pocket of sand dunes on the north side of the Assiniboine River near Carberry. Known as the Bald Head Hills, they are the essence of the park.

The heart of Hecla Park, on the island from which it takes its name, is its Icelandic history, although the ragged, rocky shoreline, which braces itself against Lake Winnipeg's frequent storms, is fascinating habitat for pelicans, gulls and many shorebirds. Moose inhabit the island. Gull Harbour Resort provides modern comfort in a wilderness setting at the island's north end, where all human activity is concentrated.

△ *The peaceful beauty of a sunset in northern Manitoba can be enjoyed many summer evenings in Clearwater Provincial Park, located east of Highway 10 between The Pas and Flin Flon.*

Birds Hill Park is near Winnipeg, a welcome place for urbanites who in summer flock to its grassy and wooded areas for relaxation. In winter, snowshoe, snowmobile and cross-country ski trails crisscross the park, while Spring Hill, its satellite just a few miles closer to the city, provides downhill skiing facilities.

If you like swimming, Grand Beach Park is the place to go. Always a resort area since the thirties, park development has brought order to what used to be a chaotic place. Sometimes the crowds who fill the park make you think it is still in chaos, but the fact of the matter is that there are interesting, well-planned trails to enjoy in a truly wonderful

△ Rolling, wooded hills, typify the countryside in Turtle Mountain Provincial Park off Highway 10 south of Boissevain.

setting that has as its focal point a magnificent beach on the east side of Lake Winnipeg.

Manitoba's one national park — Riding Mountain — is a seasoned mixture of man-made and natural beauty, a park in which the town of Wasagaming beside Clear Lake is filled to overflowing with people in summer, but where you can drive for miles in rolling hills that form the divide from north to south between two continental prairie levels. A bison herd is protected inside a huge enclosure in the middle of the hills.

Down at the Canada-United States border south of Boissevain is the International Peace Garden, a mostly

△ Left. Flags of Canada and the United States symbolize the longest unfortified border between two countries in the world. Around the flags is the beautiful International Peace Garden, straddling the cross-continental boundary between Boissevain, Manitoba, and Bottineau, North Dakota.

△ Right. Grand Beach Provincial Park is a place where in summer sailors launch out and swimmers enjoy one of Canada's finest beaches.

floral tribute to the longest unfortified border between two countries in the world.

Immediately north of the garden, adjacent to it, is Turtle Mountain Park, a place of rolling hills much less populated than others in summer.

North of there are Asessippi and Duck Mountain Parks, the first built around a reservoir that has become an excellent area for camping in lush prairie surroundings; the second a woodland which, in earlier days, was prime forest in which numerous logging operations flourished.

Still farther north up Highway 10 is Clearwater Park, which takes its name from its biggest lake. The water is so

clear you can see bottom at great depths. And still farther north is Grass River Park. The river that flows east through its heart is part of a vast network of northern waterways that were used for transportation by Western Canada's explorers, trappers and fur traders.

Finally, back in the southeast corner of the province, is Manitoba's largest park, the Whiteshell, which takes in the western edge of the great Canadian Precambrian Shield. With hundreds of rivers and lakes to choose from, many of them draining into the Winnipeg River, it is a paradise for canoeists. Resort developments are heaviest in this park as the area has been popular for Winnipeg residents for years.

△ *Left. An obsolete old lighthouse at Gull Harbour once directed Icelandic fishermen to shore at night. It is a symbol of the history of Hecla in a provincial park that takes its name from this island.*

△ *Right. Hecla Island's shoreline is eaten away each year by Lake Winnipeg's violent storms, thus turning up roots and loosening rocks. The island is a haven for a variety of waterfowl and land wildlife.*

△ Left. A creek in Riding Mountain National Park reflects the sun's radiance, then flows off to Clear Lake, focal point of the park's developed area.

△ Right. Ancient Indian rock paintings in Grass River Provincial Park marked transportation routes and reminded historic people that the sound of rushing water was interpreted to be the voice of God.

And north of the Whiteshell is Nopiming Park, Manitoba's newest summer place where human development has not yet progressed to any great degree.

Aside from the bigger parks are dozens of recreation areas and waysides throughout the province, maintained by the Department of Mines, Natural Resources and Environment. They, too, are often located to highlight one or another of Manitoba's scenic wonders. Most notable among them are Pisew Falls just off Highway 391 south of Thompson, and Wekusko Falls near the town of Snow Lake.

In all major parks, development has provided for excellent camping. Fishing is great everywhere. And

naturalists are always willing to point out things you may have overlooked before.

When it comes to outdoor enjoyment, there's no better way of learning about the natural world than experience. It's exhilarating to wake in the morning as a loon calls out from across a lake. Food tastes good when cooked outdoors, even if the hamburgers burn, or hot dogs fall into the fire and come out with ashes on them.

One of the nice things about camping in Manitoba's provincial parks is the fact that most everyone is hospitable and kind. You sometimes meet the friendliest people there. ☐

△ Canoeing at sunrise on Big Whiteshell Lake in Whiteshell Provincial Park is a lesson in soft twilight tranquility. Many routes lead in and out of the park's rivers, lakes and creeks, making it a paradise for outdoorsmen.

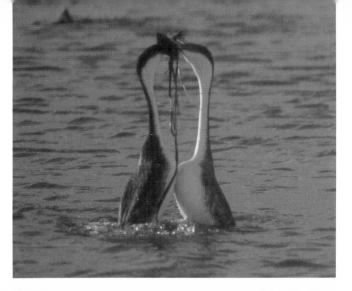

◁ A mother killdeer performs her broken-wing act to lure predators away from her nearby egg-filled nest. When she has led the enemy far enough, she suddenly bursts into the air and flies away.

▷ Western grebes paddle furiously with their feet, making them appear to be standing on water, as they perform a springtime nest-building ritual.

▽ An evening grosbeak nestles into the needles of a pine tree in winter.

The Wildlife

Spring . . . a time of new beginnings. In Manitoba's world of wildlife, marshes come alive with vibrant sounds and motions. Canada geese honk a glad-to-be-home-again note. The killdeer lures a predator away from her nest of eggs by feigning a broken wing until it is safe, then circles off into the air.

Alerted to danger, the American bittern remains motionless with neck and body stretched up, head tilted back and bill pointed skyward, making it difficult to see the bird against background vegetation. Ducks of every species abound, until hunters arrive on the scene later in the year.

More than 275 species of birds colour Manitoba's land and sky. They flock to man-made areas like Oak Hammock Marsh, just outside of Winnipeg, and to parks throughout the province.

And outside your front door, on farms and in cities, robins sing as they build their nests; woodpeckers rhythmically tap out an amazingly rapid drumbeat that makes many a city dweller stop to look up and listen during a busy day; and to a camper in the solitude of sunset, there is nothing like the haunting call of the loon.

Summer . . . a time of growth.

Sea Canaries of the North as they're called, beluga whales caper with their calves off the Hudson Bay coast.

51

△ *The Hudson Bay coast is where massive polar bears await fall ice to come in. As the bay freezes eastward from the shore near Churchill the bears go out to spend the winter at the edge of the ice to hunt for seal.*

The young ones, slate in colour, will not turn white until they reach adulthood in four to five years. Now an endangered species, these white whales are no longer harvested, and are shot just with cameras.

In the wilderness, there is much for the newborn to learn in a few short months. Black bears, residents of both deciduous and coniferous forests, are well into the task of teaching their offspring how to survive, using a variety of actions and sounds.

Alternately stalking and pouncing in the grass, red fox pups play with meadow mice that scurry along their little runways. A pair of foxes, mated for life, remain watchful

nearby. Common on farms with woodlots and roads through wilderness areas, foxes usually remain hidden from view.

Almost anywhere in southern Manitoba, coyotes may be seen, or at least heard. Both parents care for their young, beginning the task of teaching them to hunt just ten weeks after birth. Their thrilling recital of nocturnal howls may be heard particularly at nightfall or daybreak.

Amid lush growth and fertile vegetation, white-tailed deer browse peacefully to store up strength for the winter ahead.

At close range, the moose is truly an ungainly animal,

△ Upper. Two photos show goslings at left and the head of the magnificent Canada goose at right.

△ Lower. A phalarope walking along the watery edge of a dike at Oak Hammock Marsh.

△ Top left is a springtime robin, lower left a butterfly at work, and right a loon, one of the most interesting birds to inhabit Manitoba's lakes and streams. The loon's twilight call is a haunting laugh that lulls campers to sleep at dusk and awakens them at dawn.

but at a distance, what is more thrilling than to see a bull exploding from the water of a northern lake and high-stepping his way through thick marsh and over rocky terrain at a speed of 25 miles per hour?

By the end of summer, the fittest have survived and the season is changing. Life grows and goes on for more than 90 species of mammals which inhabit the forests, lakeshores and plains of Manitoba.

Fall ... a time of flight and movement.

Far north on the tundra, massive polar bears start their journey toward the sea, hungry for seal. Mothers with cubs are often seen biding their time on precambrian rock

△ *A young white-tailed deer browses in the lush new woodland growth of spring.*

overlooking Hudson Bay, or even sauntering into the streets of Churchill. When cold winds blow ice against the shore, the bears move farther out onto the frozen water to spend the winter at the edge of the ice.

Barren-ground caribou move as a huge herd from northwestern Manitoba to Baker Lake in the Northwest Territories, an awesome sight.

The snowshoe hare, most common of the rabbit family, has begun to change its coat from grayish-brown to white.

A sudden rush of movement, spurred by hidden instincts, progresses like clockwork. Time moves more quickly, and before the season is over, the geese are gone.

Winter . . . a time of solitude.

Now a sense of stillness pervades the land. Some animals lie torpid, like the black bear and raccoon. At times, the quiet is broken by an Arctic fox burrowing into the snow after a lemming. Satisfied again, the creature moves on.

A wolf howls in the distance as a snowy owl lands gently on a hedgerow.

There is life underneath the layers of snow, and movement on top, yet like the hush of a mother as her young gently sleep, winter settles in on the wildlife of Manitoba for a time . . . a short time until the cycle erupts again with the joy of birth. □

△ *Along the lakeshores and inland, seagulls are a common sight.*

◁ *The American bittern, when startled, stretches its neck and points its bill skyward, camouflaging itself in the reeds and marshy vegetation it usually inhabits.*

◁ *Winnipeg's Assiniboia Downs presents thoroughbred racing, the sport of kings, from May to September.*

△ *Shouts from the skip, and the slap and the sweep of the broom make Winnipeg, Canada's curling headquarters.*

Sports & Recreation

Traditionally, sports and recreational activities have always played vital roles in the ways in which Manitobans spend their leisure time. A variety of sports — professional or amateur, spectator or participatory — have all enjoyed tremendous support in this province over the years.

Amateur sport organizations in Manitoba are among the most active in the country. Thousands of volunteers emerge in great numbers whenever a major event is being considered. As a result, numerous national and international competitions have been hosted by the province, thereby providing communities with a legacy of facilities.

One of the most significant events in Manitoba's sport and recreation development was the staging of the Pan Am Games in 1967. Unquestionably successful, the Games brought tremendous lasting benefits. One of these was the Pan Am Pool, specially built for the event, and now considered to be one of the best of its kind in Canada. Another was the Velodrome, designed to accommodate soccer, field hockey and high-school football inside the track. Still others included a new grandstand which was added to the Winnipeg Stadium, a track and field stadium at the University of Manitoba, new courts and stands at the Winnipeg Canoe Club for tennis competitions, improvements to docks and

◁ *Blue Bombers on the line bring football fever to Manitoba fans in the Winnipeg Stadium each fall.*

△ *The Winnipeg Jets, Manitoba's entry in the National Hockey League.*

clubhouses for yachting at Gimli, improvements for equestrian events at Assiniboia Downs and Birds Hill Park, improved boxing and wrestling rings as well as dressing rooms and showers at the Winnipeg Auditorium, moveable basketball and volleyball floors in the Winnipeg Arena, and additional stands in Alexander Park for soccer games.

The Games did wonders in terms of bolstering Manitoba's image, and their success encouraged sport aficionados to vie for a number of other national and international competitions involving snowmobiling, curling and bowling, as well as various events such as the Manitoba Games and the Canada Winter Games. The latter, held in Brandon in 1979, left valuable sport facilities in their wake, including a $3.5 million sports complex which encompasses a 50-meter swimming pool, an arena, three raquetball courts, and a 400-meter outdoor speed-skating oval. Further upgrading and improvements went into a number of other facilities including Brandon's Keystone Centre, and Mount Agassiz in Riding Mountain National Park, site of the downhill skiing competitions.

It is no wonder then, that interest in recreational sport activities has thrived so well over the years, bridging the gaps between young and old, amateur and professional, and winter and summer.

Manitoba's dramatic seasons influence a dramatic diversification. Spring causes a flurry of angling action in every corner of the province as each fishing enthusiast tries to catch a limit of tasty walleye or trophy-sized northern pike.

Summer's warm temperatures bring about myriad sports that run the gamut from golf, polo and tennis on land, to whitewater rafting, canoeing and sailing on water.

The arrival of autumn, with its accompanying kaleidoscope of colours, sends people outdoors to enjoy hiking, horseback riding and cycling, while professional football fosters Blue Bomber fever at the Winnipeg Stadium.

△ *Fishing is Manitoba's most popular pastime, resulting in the sale of more than 150,000 licences per year.*

◁ *Whitewater rafting is new in the province, developed as a recreational sport in the mid-1970s. Here the rapids of the Berens River are braved by an urban crew of adventurers.*

△ *Left. Cross-country skiing has mushroomed in Manitoba as in every other province or state with snow. Trails are made and groomed regularly by staff in both country and city parks.*

△ *Right. Tobogganing is, and always has been a time for fun for children. Runs are usually built in urban areas, as is this one in Winnipeg's St. Vital Park.*

The first snowfall, rather than frightening people indoors to hibernate for the long cold winter, merely expands their horizons and changes their equipment. Downhill and cross-country skis replace waterskis; snowmobiles replace bicycles; and down-filled jackets and warm boots replace short-sleeved shirts and sneakers.

Sport fishing barely has a breather as the winter ice angler simply packs a few extra essentials like an ice auger to drill holes, before setting off to a favourite lake for the same rewarding results as in summer.

One winter sport that has experienced an unprecedented boom is cross-country skiing. The demand for

trails and equipment has risen to staggering proportions. Many of Manitoba's provincial and city parks, as well as a number of private resorts and golf courses, have responded by developing trails and, in some cases maps, to guide the skier along scenic well-marked routes.

Indoor sports, of course, continue all year, and cold weather is never an excuse for Manitobans not to stay fit.

Besides raquetball which is one of the fastest growing sports in the country, curling captures center stage as the most popular indoor activity in winter. Bonspiels and Briar results get the most ink on sports pages of Winnipeg's two newspapers as literally thousands of curlers converge on

△ *Left. One sunny day, you jockey a maverick snowmobile along a smooth winter trail, and that's when you're hooked.*

△ *Right. Snowshoeing, too, is a way of getting around, more akin to those who enjoy the stillness and solitude of winter outdoors. This setting is a scene in the Whiteshell.*

◁ *Several new riding stables have been established recently in Manitoba, making it comfortable and enjoyable to explore the hills and woodlands.*

▽ *Even at dusk, waters of Manitoba's largely shallow lakes are warm, making a twilight swim delightful.*

▷ *An unprecedented surge in outdoor recreation has sent many urbanites into the hills, rucksacks on their backs, to bask in the warmth of summer sun and discover the secrets of nature along hundreds of parkland trails.*

every available sheet of ice in the province. Manitoba's hosting of the Silver Broom in 1978, an international curling competition, gave testimony to the game's popularity. Ten countries participated in the week-long contest which saw the United States team capture the world trophy over Norway, and Manitoba become recognized as a major sport centre.

Hockey has also done its share to establish the province in the world's sports arena. Activities range all the way up the line from amateur hockey competitions to the professional world championship action of the Winnipeg Jets.

Special events and festivals provide sport enthusiasts with yet another opportunity for displaying their skills. The Flin Flon Trout Festival is known far and wide for its Goldrush Canoe Race and Fishing Derby; the Festival du Voyageur in St. Boniface sets the stage for cross-country, snowshoe and sled-dog races; and the International 500 between Winnipeg and St. Paul in Minnesota brings together top competitors for one of the biggest snowmobiling events on the continent.

Whether sporting activities take place on the green, the ice, the court, the ring or the track, Manitobans throng to them, either to see the action or be a part of it. ☐

△ French horn player in the Winnipeg Symphony, a well-known Canadian organization with good community support.

△ Historical paintings are hung in the Manitoba Archives where research is often carried out.

◁ The Winnipeg Art Gallery is a lively downtown cultural centre that sponsors exhibitions, recitals and films.

The Arts

Under the cloudless canopy of an evening summer sky, a ballerina flutters in her partner's arms as together they sink into the gentlest of embraces, delicate arms folding like petals, aristocratic necks slowly coming to rest. The music fades; the lights dim. The delighted audience claps and whistles its approval and then the ladies collapse their lawn chairs, teenagers amble off for one last game of frisbee and parents round up their children. It has been another successful performance of Ballet in the Park.

This contradictory image of tutus and running shoes, artistic perfection and hot dogs is second nature to many Manitobans. They have come to take for granted the wealth of artistic endeavours that have alternately struggled and flourished throughout the province for years. Winnipeggers are particularly fortunate. Their glittering, chandeliered Centennial Concert Hall is home for the internationally acclaimed Royal Winnipeg Ballet, the Winnipeg Symphony Orchestra and the lavish performances of the Manitoba Opera Association. Nearby, the Manitoba Theatre Centre and its innovative satellite, the MTC Warehouse Theatre, offers first-rate regional theatre, and there is always the pure energy of Winnipeg's Contemporary Dancers to take the chill off a dark January night. Every summer, Rainbow Stage's outdoor Broadway musicals are perennial family

△ A scene from Cabaret *presented by the Manitoba Theatre Centre of Winnipeg.*

△ *A dancing pair from the Royal Winnipeg Ballet, world-renowned for its performances.*

◁ *Complete with fireworks, the Winnipeg Symphony performs outdoors for thousands in Assiniboine Park, an annual fall event.*

favourites, and all year round the community-minded Winnipeg Art Gallery features everything from globe-trotting exhibits to cinema classics.

Although Winnipeg boasts the majority of the province's established artistic companies, the rest of Manitoba is by no means withering in a cultural wasteland. The citizens of Brandon, the "Wheat City", encourage their own excellent Brandon University School of Music and welcome visiting guest artists to their striking Western Manitoba Centennial Auditorium. Elsewhere in the province, ethnic choirs and dance troupes, enthusiastic art and drama clubs, co-op pottery studios, and experimental theatre groups are keeping the arts thriving at the grassroots level.

Spring music festivals bring out the best in budding students. And throughout the province are professional and church choirs that make auditoriums ring with good singing. Some groups like the Mennonite Children's Choir have toured the world to bring glory to God and fame to Manitoba.

From puppeteers to glass blowers, Manitoba's artists and artisans have become an integral part of the province, the source of long-treasured moments such as a tender pas de deux on a summer's night. ☐

△ A stained glass window in Trinity Baptist, representative of Winnipeg's many churches.

Outside back cover shows the restored Grant's Mill on Sturgeon Creek in Winnipeg's west end.